STIRRINGS OF THE WIND

STIRRINGS OF THE WIND

A Magical Treasure of Stories

Mary A. Cole

Xulon Press
2301 Lucien Way #415
Maitland, FL 32751
407.339.4217
www.xulonpress.com

© 2020 by Mary A. Cole

All rights reserved solely by the author. The author guarantees all contents are original and do not infringe upon the legal rights of any other person or work. No part of this book may be reproduced in any form without the permission of the author. The views expressed in this book are not necessarily those of the publisher.

Unless otherwise indicated, Scripture quotations taken from the New American Bible Revised Edition (NABRE). Copyright © 2010, 1991, 1986, 1970 Confraternity of Christian Doctrine, Inc., Washington, DC All Rights Reserved.

Printed in the United States of America.

Paperback ISBN-13: 978-1-6322-1215-3
eBook ISBN-13: 978-1-6322-1216-0

I dedicate this book to my wonderful family,
my Write Focus friends,
and each person mentioned in these stories
of my journey in life.

Introduction

Most of the stories in this book are true and some are a mixture of truth and fiction. It is my heartfelt prayer that when you read these pages you may be encouraged and find a deeper assurance that God's presence is closer than you can imagine. This book is meant to be read slowly and thoughtfully for the stories are meant to inspire the soul.

I hope the nature stories increase your profound awareness of God's beautiful and mysterious world. May you be blessed abundantly as you listen and see all the joys around you.

In His Love,
Mary A. Cole

Table of Contents

Stirrings of the Wind 1
Among the Trees. 3
Snowy Night 6
The Chapstick Story 8
Gift of the Storm 10
Narrow Escape 14
Hidden Meaning. 17
Golden. 20
A Kindness 23
Time Travel. 26
The Park 28
Her Love and Faith and Service 30
The Beauty of the Seasons 33
An Ode to Angels 35
The Concert in the Park 42
Slow Down 46
Hibachi Chef Story. 48
Surrender To Nature 50
To Make Their House A Home 54
The Red Wagon 57

Questions 60

Happy 62

On That Summer Night 65

Books By Jane 68

The Day of Whites 70

Clara Gilmore 74

Free 78

Picture Walk 81

A Plate of Cookies 84

Grandchildren 87

What Is Forever? 91

Stirrings of the Wind

Mother nature beckons the stirrings of the wind, so the bare trees are swaying with pure joy. I know this because it swirls around my face until it reaches deep within my heart. I see rabbit footprints in the fluffy snow but the wind soon makes them disappear. Was this little fellow filled with joy because of his warm coat? I wonder if rabbits secretly thank mother nature.

I hear a swishing sound in the distance. Is it the wind? I look up and the sky is filled with a flock of birds flying this way and that, back and forth, up and down. Their joy is unstoppable! They appear to follow one another. But who is the leader? They move as one and form a design, ever changing in the sky. How happy I am to be here in this moment of time!

The icy river is adorned with ducks as if they had somewhere special to go. Their feathers lift as they swim in the wind. The sound of their quacking makes me laugh out loud but the wind moves my voice down river. As I listen to the sound of the ducks, big white flakes blow about and their taste on my tongue delights me.

The gift of life is here in my cold breath; my lungs are full of the freshness of winter. Mother nature has given us the awakening of the senses and all the joy one can hold. Time seems to stand still.

I find myself feeling thankful for my home and heater and warm slippers and a cup of hot tea. Gifts can come in beautifully wrapped packages but gifts from mother nature in winter must be noticed, sought after and realized. Back at home, I sip my tea with joy in my heart, and I hear the stirrings of the wind.

"Praise the Lord, O my soul. O Lord, my God, you are very great, you are clothed with splendor and majesty. He wraps himself in light as with a garment. He stretches out the heavens like a tent and lays the beams of his upper chambers on their waters. He makes the clouds his chariot and rides on the wings of the wind.

Psalm 104:1, 3

Among the Trees

They say that babies are closer to heaven than anyone. A young mother was convinced of that. Her little son was eighteen months old and they experienced a magical moment together. It was a few weeks before Christmas, and time for the tradition of cutting down a Christmas tree.

The temperature was in the teens so the family bundled up for the car ride to the tree farm. The mother maintained her joy as she sang familiar carols.

Children and parents walked in the cold through the path trying to locate the finest tree. So many voices permeated the air with the sound of saws and falling timber. The aroma, Ahh! The aroma of scotch pines and balsam made everyone inhale with gusto.

Mother and baby walked among the trees and wandered away from the group. She felt like they were off in another place, another time. And yet, they could still hear voices in the distance.

Suddenly in the dusk of the evening, it started to snow large soft flakes. They fell from the sky so slowly that the baby just sat down in the snow and watched them fall. His eyes met his mothers'. They were both in awe at the gentle beauty before them. His snowsuit, scarf, and mittens turned white from head to toe. It was the first time he saw snowflakes and his face looked like an angel. She found herself sitting in the snow with him and now it was silent. It was like her ears ceased to function. The huge flakes were thick, falling ever so slowly. The mother could barely see but she sensed something moving in front of her. What was it? Something was coming toward them and she just felt inquisitive.

It was a family of white rabbits—a mama and four babies. Her little boy saw them too and he took in a deep breath in surprise. The young mother spoke softly to the bunnies and then they looked at the baby with such love, unafraid of a human voice. The mother watched and felt her little son had been blessed. Love was all around them!

She didn't know how much time had passed. Finally, the white rabbits disappeared into the snow and the sounds of Christmas returned. With peace and gratefulness in her heart, she took her baby down the path. Yes, her baby encountered a bit of heaven that day, and she vowed she would treasure this magical moment for a lifetime.

White as snow
Lord I know
You are near
My song you hear
It is your Love
My Lord above
All around us
White as snow.

Snowy Night

While dozing by the fire in my winter cabin in upper Michigan, I heard a knock at the door. I didn't understand. The blizzard was treacherous. Ten to twelve inches of snow had already fallen and I heard on the radio my surrounding roads were closed. My nearest neighbor was two long miles away.

"Who could this be? Someone's in trouble!" I thought.

I leaped off the sofa and ran to the door….another knock! I turned the dead bolt and swung the door wide open. The snow blew in the cabin helter skelter! There, standing on my doorstep, was Lois all snowy white and shivering. She was holding her sewing machine and there were totes of fabric and bags sitting in the deep snow too.

"What the heck!" I screeched. "Get in here!"

Lois is my childhood friend and we've kept in touch all these years. We used to read Bobbsey Twins books together and then graduated to Nancy Drew Mysteries. Lois taught me how to knit and sew. We were always bonded as best friends in spite of the long distance between us. Lois lives in Georgia.

We couldn't talk fast enough as she kicked off her snowy shoes. She didn't even have a heavy winter coat since she lived in such a warm area of the country. We cozied up by the fire and I made her some hot tea with a plate of cookies. I settled down to hear her story.

"I wanted to surprise you," Lois explained. "When you told me last week you'd be hanging out at your winter cabin, I decided to fly up and rent a car. I had to pay a little extra to bring my sewing machine on the plane but I don't care—I just **had** to have a visit with you. I just made it up here before they closed the roads."

I was thrilled she made the decision to come and see me and I told her so!

We opened the totes and admired all the fabrics. Lois had a keen eye for color. She brought a lilac fabric and luscious greens with deep purple underneath. There were white hydrangea with pinks, soft blues and scarlet. We had material all over the floor laughing and planning what design the quilt would be. We stopped to prepare some vegetable pizzas together and enjoyed a glass of wine.

Lois finally curled up on the sofa next to the fire. I took the lounge chair and we talked and talked for hours. Then came sleep—wonderful sleep and the wind blew the new fallen snow at the door.

The sun was peeking through the living room blinds. I opened my eyes. But where was Lois? I looked in every room. Where was her fabric and sewing machine, her shoes? NOTHING!

I knew then it had all been a dream on a snowy night.

At that moment, I heard a knock at the door…

> "A woman of noble character who can find? She is worth far more than rubies. Her lamp does not go out at night. When it snows, she has no fear for her household; for all of them are clothed in scarlet. She makes coverings for her bed; she is clothed in fine linen and purple. She is clothed with strength and dignity; she can laugh at the days to come."
>
> Proverbs 31: 10, 15, 21, 22

The Chapstick Story

Once there was a college student who signed up for classes in cold, cold January. It was 5 degrees as she entered the first night of computer class. Her sister had given her some chap stick for her wind-blown dry lips. It felt so good as she rubbed the soothing gel on her mouth.

Her new teacher had a syllabus ready for the group. The students entered and sat down at the computers. The teacher glanced at her and gave her a quizzical smile. The young women at the computers surrounding her were unfriendly, quiet and reserved.

As she followed directions, her lips felt sore again. She retrieved her chap stick in her purse and applied generously. Class ended and it was off to the bookstore for her required manuals. Oh! The line was ever so long and students waited with coats, hats and mittens in tow. She tried to be friendly. She talked to many students in line but was met with hostile stares. One more application of chap stick felt good. She decided to go home and buy her books in the morning. She was very tired.

A trip to the bathroom was necessary and she sat on the throne looking directly into the mirror. She was horrified at seeing her reflection because the chap stick was pumpkin orange! The color had seeped right under her nostrils and completely covered her chin! All the feelings went through her head and flashed from shock to embarrassment to hilarious laughter. What else could she do? Needless to say, her sister was in big trouble!

⇒ THE CHAPSTICK STORY ⇐

A quick thought went in reverse to the other students' faces when they had a good look at her. "Oh, Lord", she cried, "No wonder the strange looks!" They probably thought I was a deranged old woman pretending to be a student!

Thanks to her sister's gift of pumpkin chap stick, she would have to face those students the next evening! Maybe they'll forget all about it, she mused.

Off to class she went, still wondering why every woman kept silent about her unusual mouth that evening. Maybe the students felt a little afraid of a person who looked like this! Well, she walked into the second computer class acting like nothing ever happened! She was me.

> "Live in harmony with one another; be sympathetic, love others, be compassionate and humble."
>
> 1 Peter 3: 8

Gift of the Storm

I stood at the window and watched the snowflakes fall. I felt myself shivering deep within and thinking that I just needed a cup of hot tea and my fleecy robe. The snow was blowing in high drifts at the door wall and the weatherman gave a stormy forecast for the rest of the evening.

I made my Lemon Lift tea, donned my robe and started the long and tedious job of putting Christmas decorations away. There were strings of pearls and hand crocheted snowflakes, bubble lights and sweet angels. One particular angel was my very favorite. His sparkling wings still glowed with great beauty. He held a violin and I imagined him playing his instrument skillfully many times in the past. I was just about to place him in his box when the most unusual thing happened. I heard something. Was it the wind?

No, it was a very faint sound quite close to me. I wanted to put it in the back of my mind, but the sound persisted until I was sure it was a "voice." Yes! It *was* a voice!

The voice said to me in a whisper, "I have a question to ask you."

I was absolutely silent for a moment. I heard the voice a little louder this time.

"I have a question to ask you."

The wind howled outside and I could see the snow blowing sideways with great force. Suddenly, with a flash of brilliancy and a magnificent beacon of light, the angel stood in my room as tall as me! He was holding his violin with great care and he looked at me with a gentle and loving gaze. I stared at him and reached behind me for the sofa so I could sit down.

"A question?" I asked as my body trembled.

He said, "*I do* have a question to ask you.

"Do you know that you may walk in newness of heart? Today, this moment your spirit will bloom if you believe in the miracle within you."

"Miracle within me? Newness of my heart? What does that mean, sir?" I queried.

He looked at me. His eyes were filled with kindness. My mind and my spirit spoke aloud.

"You have persuaded me, sir, I do believe," I said.

"Place your hand on my violin," he beckoned.

As I did so, a soft glow touched my fingers and I felt a tingling sweetness in my bones. He smiled and I smiled too. A moment passed and I watched in awe as a new violin formed from his. I took the bow in my hand and I played my very own instrument with grace and beauty and I knew in an instant *there was* a newness in my heart.

As I turned around to say "thank you" to my friend, he was gone. I searched under the tree for the box and found my angel neatly tucked away.

I whispered to him that I would use my gift with great joy and I thought I saw a sweet smile on his angelic face.

My cup of tea was cold, but my heart was warm and overflowing. I stood at the window and watched as the snowflakes continued to fall. I picked up my treasured violin and played in rhythm to the falling snow.

> "In our journey in life, we are gifted with a spirit to bloom. Miraculous newness can come to us in the most unexpected ways."

Unknown

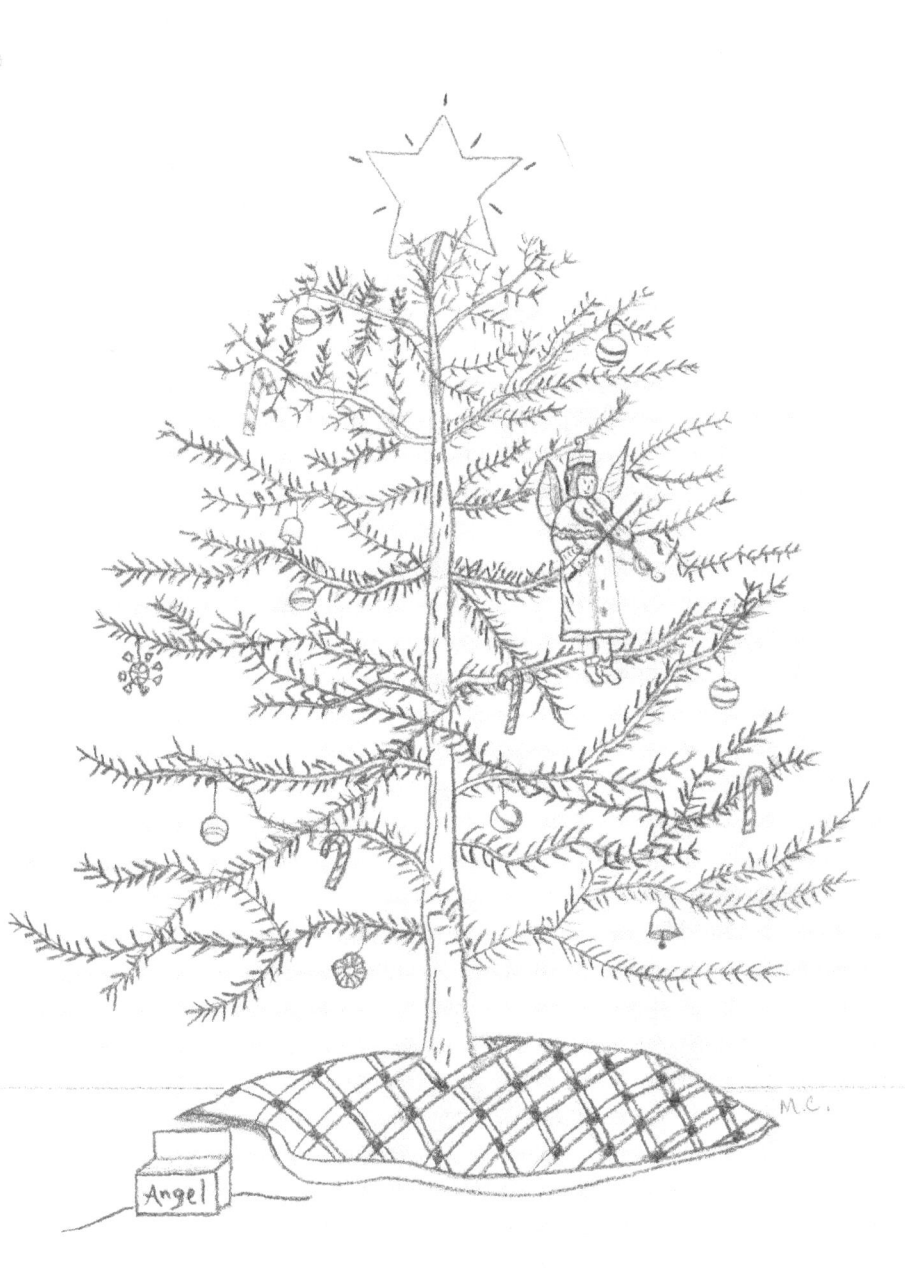

Narrow Escape

The fresh snow covered the brown slush making everything new again. People just expected a mid-April snow in this most northern state. But last December, the families in Lakewood North Dakota prepared for the winter blast with a quaver in their souls. There wasn't a family in Lakewood who didn't hear the story of Fred's narrow escape the winter before. A lesson was learned by all and Fred's name was etched in the hearts of the townspeople for many years to come. Here is his story.

Fred was very well liked because of his generous spirit and good sense of humor. He had plenty of work to do in Lakewood, North Dakota because people trusted in his ability to fix just about anything. Folks welcomed him in their homes giving samples of warm apple pie, a pot of chili or deep chocolate brownies in exchange for a new faucet installed, or the like. Smiles and gentle kindness filled the rooms wherever he went. He always seemed to have enough money for everything he needed.

Yes, he was talented. Fred could install new cupboards, repair farm equipment and work well with other men building barns. He could paint inside and outside a home with perfection; he played the piano at parties and festivals, and could teach a boy to fish. If a woman in Lakewood needed a new floor in her kitchen, Fred just seemed to know about it. He'd get a few friends to help and in one afternoon the job was done. Was it possible an entire town turned to excellence in their daily work because of one man? Some people seemed to think so.

Narrow Escape

That winter, they almost lost Fred. It was late on a Saturday evening and a snowstorm was approaching from the north. Fred had been ice fishing at Devil's Lake but didn't even catch a little perch. He wished George could have joined him but the poor fellow broke his ankle while hunting. Fred didn't mind being alone that day. His thoughts were centered on the fish to be caught. He had to keep poking the ice with the stick he carried because the opening covered with ice so quickly. Fred didn't notice the black clouds, but soon his eyes glanced to the sky when the wind almost lifted him off the ice. He knew he didn't have much time to get back home. The snow came down in swirls of white, accumulating at record speed. Fred packed up his gear and headed toward the road but all he could see were spinning white drifts. The warm clothing and quilted body suit he wore were a gift from George. He remembered the elation he felt at Christmas when he opened the box. He thought about George, his friends, his life.

He had to find a way out of this storm! Survival was on his mind now. Fred gave his best effort to light a fire. Trying to find kindling was impossible. The wind howled; he couldn't light a match, and removing his gloves to do so would be a dangerous step!

He knew he must have been walking in circles. Fred wondered if he told anyone he was going fishing. No, George didn't even know. He felt angry with himself for being so foolish. The efforts at making an icy igloo proved fruitless because the snow was soft. It felt like several hours had passed. He needed to rest, and yet, his instincts warned him! *Keep moving!* A prayer to God rose from his lips and continued with persistent pleas for help. Suddenly, there before him was a mystical mirage. He blinked over and over again. The white moose stood still. Could it be a snow moose? It was a male, probably 400 pounds. His palmate antlers were enormous; this was odd since males shed their antlers in winter to preserve strength. This great beast looked directly into his soul. It was as if he was telling Fred something. Confusion and fear pierced the man's heart. There were tales of strange things happening at Devil's Lake. Then the most unusual thing happened. This huge animal knelt down in the snow falling onto its side. Fred knew the beauty of what was happening. He walked over to the beast and lay down next to him. The heat from the body of this moose was a great relief. The storm raged on, but Fred was kept warm! He could hear the breathing of the great elk, steady with each inhale, exhale.

It was morning. The sun shone brightly on the sparkling new fallen snow. Fred realized his life had been spared, but the great beast lay dead. Fred whispered a word of thanks to this generous friend in nature and found his way back home.

He told his story at the community hall the next night and his friends urged him to return to the spot where the moose lay. It was George who suggested to use his snow truck plow and take the animal for meat. Fred hesitated. In time, they convinced him the moose had the intention of giving himself away; sharing the frozen meat with the families of the community was honorable.

The silence of the men was eerie when they returned. The great moose was gone! No one questioned Fred's credibility. Fred was alive. He believed his prayer had been answered. He learned his lesson well.

Now, spring was on its way. Things would be all right again.

> "Every whispered prayer is heard by the Lord God of Hosts."
>
> Unknown

Hidden Meaning

I tried to close it and lock it, as I struggled in desperation for its comforting locked security pushing hard against the door with my whole body. It HAD to shut and stay shut! It HAD to lock.

"Why won't you close?" I asked myself in panicked frustration. I continued to push with mounting determination as fear and anxiety rose with every passing second.

Suddenly, without warning, the door knob fell through to the other side with a "clunk" on the cement. No wonder it wouldn't lock! I was peering through the hole where all security now vanished. My family had left long ago. I was dreadfully alone. It was dusk and I felt the wind picking up whipping through the gaping hole in my door. I dashed outside to pick up the pieces to see if I could fix it. Oh! What was I thinking?

Now the door was stuck like glue and I couldn't get back inside! I placed my hand in the hole and gave the door a mighty tug. But something or someone had a hand on my shoulder. I turned around still using all my strength to get the door opened. The darkest and extremely tall form was behind me gripping my shoulder! I couldn't see his face. He reminded me of the spirit from Scrooge's apparition.

"Who are you? What do you want?" I screamed.

All I could hear was the wind. The gust was cold and hurt my ears and bit my cheeks. Tears came from my eyes but this creature behind me was completely silent. His huge blackness moved back-— away from me and vanished into the night. I felt such relief, nothing like I have ever experienced before. My hand instinctively went to the door and it easily opened!

There before me was the most exquisite color-filled garden I had ever seen in my life. There were red, yellow and white rose bushes, hibiscus bushes in full bloom, buttercups and Queen Ann's lace, red geraniums and purple violets. I wasn't inside the house any longer. Where did this lush garden come from? I laughed and laughed! What an abrupt change in my feelings!

I took a step forward and heard piano music—my mother's tunes from long ago. I hurried to the direction of the familiar melody and saw my mom playing, smiling with her right shoe off to the side. Her stocking foot moved to the pedals with precision. Everything was so strange because she didn't see me even when I stood beside the piano ready to give her a hug. I could smell the fragrance of the flowers and I said, "hello mom" but there was no response from her. I turned to look back at the garden and a fog so thick covered the entire area.

All I wanted to do was lock my door. Lock it—shut it—make it stay shut. Why was I so fearful? Why all the panic and anxiety? Was it a blessing my door knob fell through? Was it a blessing the dark figure had his hand on my shoulder? I *know* it was a blessing to see the flower garden and I felt very blessed to see my mom so happy. I also knew what my lesson was…to let go of these imaginary fears. No matter what things look like, everything will turn out all right. At least I hoped so!

I heard the sound of the snow plow on my street. I opened my eyes, threw back the covers and sat up with the realization I had a meaningful dream! Most of the time, I forget my dreams as I awake, but not this time! I grabbed my notebook and pen and started to write everything down. When I was finished, my thoughts turned to interpretation. What is the meaning for me behind this dream?

I was unable to lock my door—did I have a fear of my safety in real life?

The doorknob fell out on the other side—did I believe I was loosing control? The hand of the dark figure was on my shoulder—did I feel threatened or was he there to protect me? (no matter what he looked like).

The garden was back inside of my home—I was actually quite safe all along in this dream? I heard my mom's piano music—I know I felt comfort at her joy. The fog covered over the garden—did I finally see clearly I was covered over in God's Love?

I had watched "The Christmas Carol" the day before my dream. Perhaps that foreboding figure of the future was lingering in my mind when I fell asleep. And, actually, he was there in Scrooge's life to teach him an important lesson and protect him from a terrible fate!

Someone once told me that fear stands for:

<u>F</u>alse <u>E</u>vidence <u>A</u>ppearing <u>R</u>eal. Sometimes, a dream seems to be a wonderful thing to remember!

> "In a dream, in a vision of the night when deep sleep falls on men as they slumber in their beds, he may speak in their ears and give them warnings to turn from wrongdoing and keep them from pride."

Job 33: 15, 16, 17

Golden

The small lake was completely frozen. I sat quietly by my bedroom window and placed my red shawl around my shoulders. The snow was about four feet deep but the young fathers cleared away a nice sized skating area on the ice for the children. All was quiet. It was 7 am. I went downstairs to prepare my tea. My routine fell into place—tea kettle on, loose tea in the strainer, retrieve my favorite blue mug and wait for the whistling. I scrambled my eggs, buttered the toast and let my tea steep.

As I gathered my meager meal and sat down at the table, I saw before me a golden hammer and another pretty blue cup! It appeared to be filled with water. Was I seeing things? Where did these things come from? Then I thought of my sister. She must have dropped in late last night and left them on my table. Was it a little joke? I looked up and there on the wall in my kitchen was a note that read:

> *"Go ahead, make your choice. The outcome will decide whether you're ready or not."*

But this didn't look anything like my sisters' handwriting. For some reason, I felt it was all right; I would play along with the little game. I was very much drawn to that golden hammer. So I picked it up and instantly the pretty blue cup and its contents vanished from my sight!

"Whoa!" I whispered. "I guess I made my choice. OK! That's it!"

I threw my red shawl aside. I don't understand why, but I got my coat, hat and boots on, put a bit of my toast and some twine in my coat pocket and headed outside near the skating rink with the golden hammer in my hand.

In the cold, I saw wood, insulation and a large box of golden nails sitting in the snow. I instinctively knew I *must* build an ice shanty with the materials set before me. As if by a magnet, a few dads in the neighborhood came by to help. With miraculous speed and efficiency, the ice shanty was complete in a few hours resting several yards from the rink. The men left as quietly as they came so I stepped inside the newly built shanty and spotted a golden saw hanging on a golden nail. I used the saw to cut a hole in the ice and the entire abode glowed in a golden hue. I sat on the ice, beheld the beauty of my surroundings, and silently gave thanks from the depths of my being.

With awe of the moment, I looked down to see the golden hammer and the golden saw disappear just as the cup on my kitchen table did. Compelled to go on, I took the twine from my coat pocket, attached the bit of toast and slowly lowered it into the frigid water. Waiting patiently, I fully expected to catch a fish. The golden glow in the shanty lingered so my mind and body were completely at peace. With a supernatural yank of the twine, a small golden fish flopped on the ice and looked at me. I noticed something else. This little fellow had a treasure in its mouth— (and it wasn't the bit of toast!) I gently opened its mouth and pulled out a golden ring. As I placed it on my finger I noticed it fit perfectly. I looked intently at this unusual fish, and I heard, not in audible words, but in spirit to spirit communion:

> *"You've been given a gift. By wearing this ring, you will know you are in the right place at the right time doing the right thing for the people in your life in just the right way. Even if you take this ring off your finger, you will always have a*

> *reverence for life. Always be thankful as you were when you sat quietly on the ice. You are ready to wear this ring because you chose the golden hammer."*

I expressed a silent "thank you" and slipped the golden fish back into the water and watched him swim away.

I heard children's voices. I ran to the house to don my skates. I was in the right place at the right time. I would make myself a fresh cup of tea with my lunch but I stood there in wonderment and thought, "What would've happened if I chose that pretty blue cup of water"?

> "One of the most graceful things a person can do is to wait for the right time—and the right place will follow."
>
> Unknown

A Kindness

A long time ago I experienced a kindness given to me by a woman my own age. I will always remember her. I will always remember my feelings and the circumstances that brought about this gift from the past. It was springtime and Easter was approaching.

My oldest son had been in preschool since September. The moms took turns being the teachers' assistant a few days a month. This program was less expensive and to me it was important that my little son develop friendships with children his own age. We lived paycheck to paycheck and money was spent on necessities only. Even getting a haircut was a luxury.

In order to make some funds for the preschool, they hosted a little flea market. One of the tables contained items for an auction. We were to buy a ticket for a quarter, place our name on the ticket and the winner would be drawn for that particular item. Something so unique and beautiful to me caught my eye on that auction table! I screeched with delight when I held one in my hand. They were a set; four hand crocheted chicks for Easter in pink, blue, orange and yellow. They each sat on a white plastic egg which filled up their little bodies. I loved them instantly and looked in my purse for a quarter. But with a heavy wounded heart, I found no money at all. I mentally gave up my chance to own them.

One of the other moms must have been watching me. She came up to me and said, "I have an extra quarter," and held out the coin for me.

I looked at her and said, "Oh no, I couldn't."

When she insisted I said, "What if I win them? I should give them to you since it's your quarter?"

She said with a smile, "If you win them you keep them, you really love those chicks!"

I do not know if the person who drew my name knew what had happened. Was the drawing rigged or did God just want to bless me? I don't know. But my name was drawn and those dear chicks were mine. Can you imagine the joy in my heart when they were placed in a little brown bag and handed to me? I must have said, "thank you" a dozen times to the dear mom who gave me that quarter and I'm sure her heart was bursting with joy just watching my reaction.

There is someone else in this story as well. It is the person who sat quietly in a chair with a crochet hook perhaps following the directions of a pattern. I appreciate her and each stitch made with love.

I have treasured these chicks and displayed them proudly in my home every Easter for many years. Children are instinctively drawn to them as they adorn my basket. Recently, I brought them to show n' tell for my 4 year old Sunday school class and the children reacted as I expected. They <u>all</u> wanted to hold one. My gift from the past just keeps on giving.

"Love is patient, love is kind."

1 Corinthians 13:4

Time Travel

*I*f I could travel back in time I would like to see Jesus of Nazareth. My name would still be Mary and I would follow Jesus everywhere. What excitement it would be to see the lame walk, the deaf to hear and the blind to see!

Would I be in the crowd when the woman touched his cloak and her bleeding ceased? Would I be near enough to hear his words, "Who touched me?" When Jesus taught the crowds from the boat would my heart melt with love and joy for the way he spoke? Would I want his eye to catch mine so he would instinctively know I wanted to follow him with all my being for all time? Would his parables make me ponder for days, and keep me awake at night?

Would I be a friend of Martha, Mary and Lazarus? Perhaps, like Martha, I'd cry at Lazarus' funeral and wished Jesus was present in Bethany when Lazarus was ill to prevent this tragedy from happening. I wonder what it would feel like to see Lazarus step out of the tomb all wrapped in burial cloths.

I think I would have baked Jesus a sweet raisin cake and brought it to his house for breakfast one day—anything—just to be near him. Would I have known the mother of the little girl who died? Perhaps I was the little girls' nurse. Would I try to console the mother and then watch Jesus come into the house? I would hear him say, "Fear is useless, what is needed is trust. She's not dead. She's asleep." And then, I would watch him take the girls' hand and say, "Little girl, get up." With awe and unbelief, I would see how she stood up and hear Jesus say to her parents, "Give her something to eat."

Time Travel

Maybe I would be one of the lepers that Jesus made whole. Did my family abandon me because of the dreaded disease? My gratefulness to Jesus would be outpouring as I thanked him over and over with tears running down my cheeks. I would finally be accepted!

You never know, maybe I would be the woman caught in adultery ready to be stoned. After Jesus silently wrote in the sand, all the accusers left and his forgiving words would ring in my heart for my entire life. "Has anyone condemned you?" "No one, sir." "Nor do I condemn you. Go and sin no more."

My only thought is the dreadful arrest, trial and crucifixion. Three days of misery and anguish and then—Sunday morning! Maybe I would be the Mary that saw him in the garden. Would I be the one to see the angels in dazzling robes telling me, "He is not here, He is risen!"

If I could go back in time this is where I'd like to be—where perfect Love walked on the earth.

> "There are still many other things that Jesus did, yet if they were written about in detail, I doubt there would be room enough in the entire world to hold the books to record them.
>
> John 21: 25

The Park

Watching and listening to children at play
The park lets me live in the moment.
A small boy shouts, "Dad, another dog!"
The father responds with kindness in his voice.
"Yah! It's a cocker spaniel," and they stroll to the fountain.

I see a child with thick glasses
The park calls me to live in the moment.
This brave boy climbs the ropes skillfully
The bars are high in the air yet he swings with ease.
He wears his blue baseball cap backwards.

There are happy children everywhere
The park woos me to live in the moment.
A girl ties her jacket around her waist,
But as she climbs high the wind plays tricks.
The hood of her jacket balloons out—her derrière is huge and blue!

A child is carrying a Tupperware bowl.
The park permits me to live in the moment.
He comes toward me wearing his Detroit Tigers shirt,
But stops at the water fountain and fills his cup.
He walks back carefully and proudly presents his gift to the golden retriever. The dog laps it up.

A plaid blanket is arranged on the grass.
The park beckons me to live in the moment.
A young couple lying on their tummies

The Park

Discuss something quietly and live in the moment too.
The red cooler holds down a corner of the blanket,
And a quart of Squirt on the other side.

I hear the train whistle near the railroad tracks.
The park allows me to live in the moment.
My ears are cold; the breeze is strong and messing up my hair.
But I see a little girl roller skating.
Her arms are extended balancing herself.
"Mom, look at me!" she shouts.

A fast-food bag is being carried to a picnic table
The park lets me live in the moment.
Mother says, "Chocolate chip and peanut butter—those are yours."
The little one takes a big bite.
I see their smiling faces. I hear the sound of the chickadee, the children laughing.
The park pleases me to live in the moment.

"Any day spent watching living souls at the park is a good day, yes, even a gift from God."
Mary Cole

Her Love and Faith and Service

*M*yla walked down a street with neat little houses on each side and she heard dogs barking in the distance. It was March—a chilly day—she pulled her hood up and buttoned the tab, nice and snug.

Myla's joy was established in her faith in God. Her daily prayer time in the morning and evening gave her an authentic spirituality that surprised other women her age. She wasn't concerned about the social system of the day, about an invitation to go somewhere or to do what everyone else was doing or wearing the latest expensive fashion to impress others. No, she had other more important things to think about.

She carried her briefcase with hope in finding just the right person to tell. Hope was what she needed most.

But this day, her thoughts turned to worries. She remembered how in the past she tried to complete a difficult task and it seemed discouragement and failure got in the way. It held her back—made her question her own endeavors. Her excitement became dulled. The question arose—Should she go on and persist with this? She felt this was happening all over again.

Myla had seen with her own eyes the poorest of the poor on a pilgrimage overseas and she knew her life had changed. She was introduced to a worldwide program where children and the elderly were given assistance to ease their poverty by sponsorship.

Her Love and Faith and Service

Myla was driven. She believed if people back home were just informed of this…

But it was a monumental task. And here she was, going door to door in the cold with her briefcase of forms. She hadn't been very successful lately and she was feeling desperately sad.

"Please Lord, can you help me out here?" she whispered.

Myla went up the steps of a home and knocked. An old woman answered with a smile and greeting.

"Come in," she said. "What's your name?"

No one had ever asked her to come in from the cold before. She sensed a peace in this home, a welcome change. As Myla opened her briefcase and explained sponsorship, the old woman had a light in her eyes and said,

"I have been assisting children in the Philippines for years—I'll share with you my folder of letters and photos. What a little miracle we have here! Of the hundreds of streets and homes in this city, you have come to *my* house.

Myla felt like this *was* indeed a miracle and the two talked about their journey of faith in Christ for some time. Then, the old woman said, "I can't afford to sponsor another child but I want to give you a gift. It's a book of prayers and scriptures. Now, when is your birthday Myla?"

"February 19th,' she said.

"Let's see what it says."

As the old woman read aloud, Myla was filled to the brim with tender emotions.

> "Revelation 2: 19
> "I know your deeds—your love and faith and service—as well as your patient endurance; I know also that your efforts of recent times are greater than ever." Myla's eyes filled with tears and the prayerful message continued…
> "Dear Lord,
> This is such an uplifting word of encouragement. You are always by my side, so You know my deeds, my love, faith and service. Even if I feel unproductive and have to wait with patience You are always near. I see the love, patient endurance and kind deeds of Your beloved Son, Jesus. May this circle of faith continue in me to glorify You. Amen."
> "One of the highest human duties is the duty of encouragement…We have a Christian duty to encourage one another. Many a time a word of praise or thanks or appreciation or cheer had kept a man on his feet. Blessed is the one who speaks such a word."
> William Barclay

With tears streaming down her face, Myla said, "Thank you, Oh, thank you, this is a perfectly amazing gift from God!"

Hugs were given to newfound friends and Myla was renewed in soul and spirit. She left the old woman's home and walked with pure joy down the street with her book clutched to her heart.

> "Prayer is our humble answer to the inconceivable surprise of living.
>
> Rabbi Heschel

The Beauty of the Seasons

There is distinctive beauty in the wintertime. I watch the snow accumulate at my door wall on a Saturday afternoon. The white flakes fall from the sky swirling, blowing about and drifting into smooth piles in the yard. Early Sunday morning a great beauty awaits. The sun shines and the snow is sparkling. It is untouched by rabbit footprints. My thoughts wander back to another time, another place, another winter.

I see an upstairs window. It is covered with swirls of ice. There before me are forms of great majestic mountains. The colors of light blue and soft violet appear and I am enlightened and transformed. Childhood memories of such great beauty will always be remembered. Yes, there is distinctive beauty in the wintertime.

The weather in spring teases me in anticipation of great change. The beauty of green new life peeks through the remaining snow. The crocus, daffodils and tulips will soon appear and their colors will remind me of God's very own palette. Sometimes, it rains several days in a row. The scent of worms on the sidewalk and the muddy soil permeate the air. I drink my herbal tea sitting on the sofa and then open the window for a while. I hear the gentle rain drops more clearly now. O, thank you, dear God, for the beauty of spring!

Summertime produces its very own artistry. If I am committed to being carefully aware, the beauty of this season produces great joy that continues for years to come. I take photographs of flowers, summer homes, lakes and smiling faces at the beach. They are subjects for future oil paintings. Flowered and beaded flip flops don the feet of young girls. The Rose of Sharon trees bloom at a steady pace and the hummingbirds dart away after a drink of red sweetness. In the campground at night time there are billions of stars. Family and friends gaze and discuss their beauty singing old tunes. I appreciate summertime beauty.

The fall is filled with beauty and speaks a language of departure, release. One last breath of life's color and the leaves succumb to death's door. I have walked down the street on a brisk fall morning in an old neighborhood. It is the only season I hear the crunch of red and golden leaves beneath my feet. This ritual has always reminded me of eating delicious potato chips. Oak trees drop their millions of acorns along the path near the lake. The beauty is in the wonder of it all. Even the marigolds wither but the beauty is contained in the seeds for next year.

There is much beauty in hiding away indoors to sew, read, write or paint on a brisk fall day. And yet, it is the prime season for apples and visiting the cider mill. Many families enjoy the last of the tomatoes, squash and zucchini. There is beauty everywhere.

> "Put your hope in God who richly provides us with everything for our enjoyment.
>
> 1 Timothy 6:17

An Ode to Angels

AN ANGEL ENTERS

Alone in the hospital elevator
My heart is heavy, my husband is dying.
The door opens; an angel enters.
Her skin, her face is so smooth—unforgettable.
Her clothes are ancient but well-kept.
Her eyes are sweet, soft and kind.
Suddenly she speaks to me.
"Do you believe in angels?" she asks with her angel voice.
Without hesitation I reply,
"Oh Yes, I DO believe in angels."
My certainty satisfies her and she beams.
She exits on the third floor and disappears.
I feel somehow lifted, not so wounded, renewed in spirit.
"Thank you", I whisper. "Thank you."

I LOOK UP

I am alone,
I feel content, safe, as I grocery shop.
My cart fills up quickly.
I am choosing yogurt, last on my list.
For some reason I look up.
There before me is a man, his eyes glued to mine.
He walks slowly toward me,
We are locked in this moment of time.
He stops, his eyes still penetrating my soul.
He says, "Hello, how are you?"
I return the greeting and we both pause.
Joy abounds! We are happy to meet.
He disappears from my sight.
I return to the yogurt aisle
Elated, so content, happy and free and not so alone anymore.

BABY, BEAUTIFUL BABY

Beautiful baby granddaughter on my lap.
She pats her bottle as if it were a friend.
Suddenly she sits up.
This baby looks to the hallway.
I cannot get her attention.
She stares at the empty space.
Such a huge smile on this baby's face.
She waves and waves her hand in the air!
I see nothing.
She sees an angel.
We are surrounded and filled with love.

THE WHITE CLOUD

We celebrate with family at the lake.
We sit and chat outside in the shade.
Cousins together,
Remembering beloved mothers gone to heaven.
But troublesome words surface our lips.
"I wonder if she's OK?"
"If only I could have helped her more."
"I wish I knew if she was happy."
In agreement, we ask God for a sign,
And wonder if its permissible to ask for such a thing.
Suddenly, we both look up.
The sky is blue.
The white cloud is astonishing!
It's a perfect angel.
Soaring above us, robe flowing
and wings celestial.
A sign of certainly our mothers are safe, still loving us.
We feel gloriously happy, free from fears.
This lingering angel stays—
We eat at the picnic table laughing and liberated,
Joyful and blessed by this angel above us!

DRIVING

I was driving down the street
I saw a man on a bicycle
In the corner of my right eye.
I stopped!
He zoomed in front of my car.
Angels unseen with perfect directions
Saved the man and my tender heart.
O Lord! Thank you for your angels.
A few seconds earlier and …
But it was not allowed to happen.
Gratefulness, gratefulness
Gratefulness for God's angels.

SWEET SLEEP

A cold winter January evening
I was sleeping in my chair.
Half awake, half asleep, the TV voices subdued.
I sensed, I felt, I knew
Someone was in the room with me.
Someone there, someone nice,
Someone protecting me. It certainly was an angel of the Lord.
I whispered, "Thank you, thank you. I love you too."

Messengers, protectors, comforters, angels are among us.

> "Then I looked and heard the voice of many angels numbering thousands upon thousands and ten thousand times ten thousand. They encircled the throne and all cried out, "Worthy is the Lamb that was slain to receive power and wisdom and strength, honor and glory and praise! Revelation 5: 11

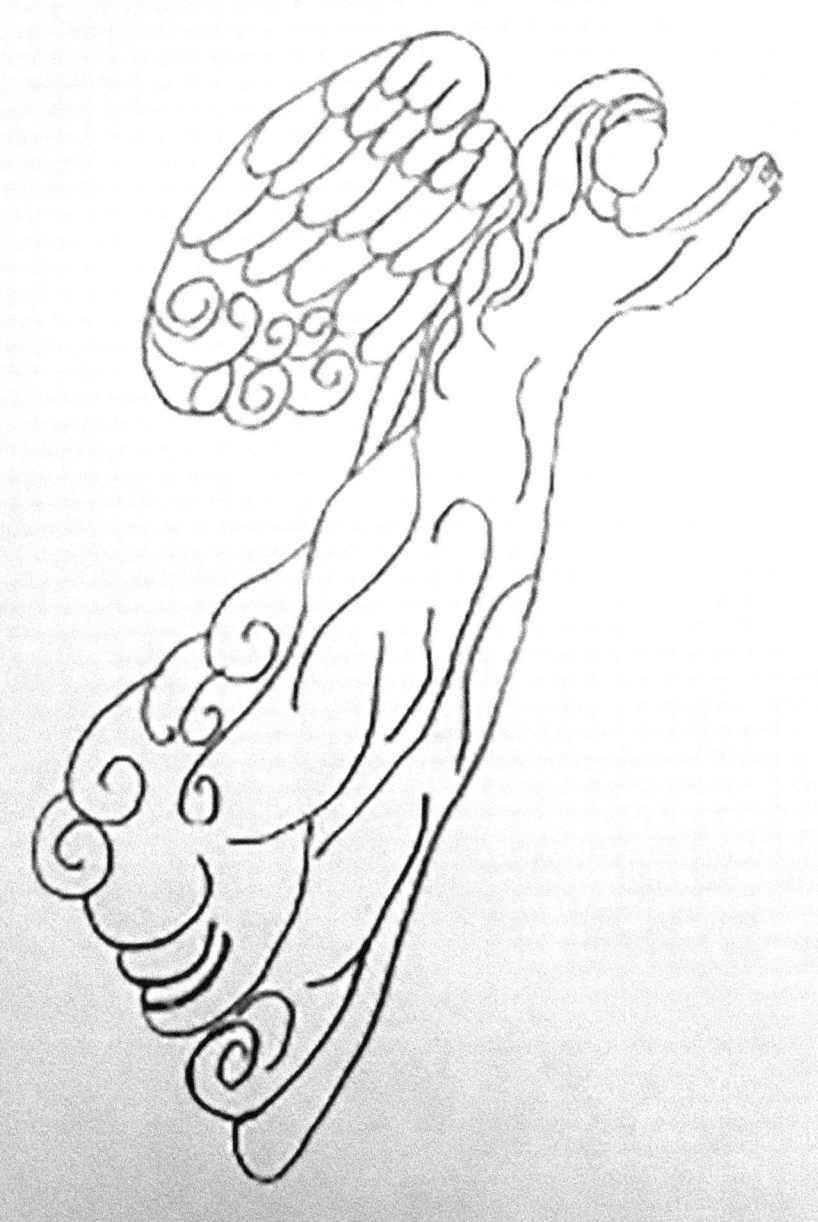

The Concert in the Park

One glorious summer evening, I was invited to a concert in the park. My friends and I brought lawn chairs, wine, snacks and a couple of blankets in case it got chilly after sundown. We had been looking forward to this event and arrived early to get a good lawn seat.

Before the concert began, my focus turned to two little children. I guessed with my motherly instinct they were about two and a half years old. The little girl was wearing a long old-fashioned dress with smocking above the waist. The little boy wore overalls and appeared to be a wee farmer. At first they didn't seem to know one another but then I watched these two for quite some time playing peek-a-boo behind an enormous tree.

Without warning, my eyesight became fuzzy, and my hearing had ceased to function. The aroma of sweet lilies of the valley filled the air. Then I heard the voices of what I interpreted as angels singing praises to God. I felt completely at peace. To my surprise, I could hear these lovely little children speaking great wisdom to one another.

My first thought was that they had been on earth hundreds of thousands of years and had gained insight in all matters of worth. Were there such things as "old souls?" I was not alarmed at the situation I was in; I succumbed to the moment and listened intently.

"Love's domain is so simple isn't it?"

"Yes, practice giving thanks."

The Concert in the Park

They gently touched one another's faces.

"And I thank OUR MAKER for you, my friend, and I receive you and bless you."

"And I bless you as well!"

They were holding hands now.

"Look at all the dear people here. All belong to our LOVING CREATOR and He wants only their greatest good."

They sat down on the blanket facing one another as they continued.

"Look up, look to the left and right and see the delights of this moment!"

Still holding hands they looked up at the evening sky.

"Imagine if everyone knew His love never leaves us."

They both sighed.

I could barely hear the music of the instruments in the park. The singing of a love song was very far away. I thought the concert must have begun but I wanted to hear more of the children! I concentrated on the two little cherubs with all my might.

They were sitting together with their backs to the stage and chatted on.

"What is your assignment?" asked the boy.

"I must see what is really important in this life", she responded.

In unison, they spoke the very same words…

"What is really important is invisible to the eye." They giggled.

I watched as he appeared to be inhaling the scent of the lawn.

"Every blade of grass has its angel that bends over it and whispers, "Grow, Grow!"

They both hesitated in a comfortable silence.

"I must learn to dwell among the beauties and mysteries of the earth so I will never be alone or weary of life," he said with dignity.

It was as if she had asked him unconsciously what <u>his</u> assignment was. Again there was silence.

The voice of the heart is the true voice, I pondered. How could these children be gifted with such grace?

I found myself looking up to the heavens as they had done, contemplating all I had seen and heard. I had no thought of how much time had passed.

Ever so slowly, I let go and allowed clarity of the melodies in the park. The trees swayed and seemed aglow with spiritual awareness to me. My friend nudged me and handed me a glass of wine.

"Hey, are you here or somewhere else?"

I guess I gave her a blank look. She just continued to pass around our treats.

I looked for the children but they were gone. This didn't surprise me, but I found myself wanting to search for a sign of their presence.

The Concert in the Park

At the concert's end, I instinctively walked over to the tree where the children sat. Carved on the trunk were these words, "Friends Forever".

> "On one occasion Jesus spoke thus: Father, Lord of heaven and earth, to You I offer praise; for what You have hidden from the learned and the clever You have revealed to the merest children."
>
> Matthew 11: 25

Slow Down

There are certain events in life one never forgets. Perhaps you are thinking of a monumental birthday, wedding day, the birth of a child or a spectacular vacation. This unusual episode is different, but oh so memorable.

I am certain God is present with us, protecting us from harms way. He knows the length of our appointed days here on earth and apparently makes sure we have the chance to fulfill them. It was spring of 1975. I was a young mother and I tried to do my best day by day. It was time to go grocery shopping so I loaded the car with my little ones and sang a favorite children's song. I drove down the street and suddenly I heard a man's clear voice say to me, "Slow down."

I wondered if my children heard the voice too. I didn't pay attention to the warning and just kept driving along.

Again, I heard a man's voice say "SLOW DOWN" with emphasis this time. My thoughts argued with the voice and I said, "Why should I slow down?"

Again, I heard this firm warning, now in a loud voice, "SLOW DOWN!!"

Finally, giving in, I said, "OK, I'll slow down!"

At that moment a car whizzed in front of me at a high speed and I knew someone was surely watching over me and the boys.

Slow Down

Trembling in fright after seeing that speeding car, I kept saying, "thank you, thank you" all the way to the grocery store.

It occurred to me the speeding driver ignored the stop sign and probably just had a fight with a family member and took off in his car in a fit of rage. I also realized this simple conversation between this voice and myself was all completed in about 12 seconds.

I don't know why some people are involved in terrible accidents. Is it just being in the wrong place at the wrong time? My heart pours out compassion for those who lost a loved one in a car accident. All I know is I felt it important to share this story because for some reason my sons and I were spared.

I hope I will always remember to obey those instincts and not be stubborn doing things my own way. If I WAS stubborn that day, my children and I wouldn't be here to tell about my timely messenger.

> "The Lord your God is with you, he is mighty to save. He will take great delight in you, he will quiet you with his Love, he will rejoice over you with singing.
>
> Zephaniah 3: 17

Hibachi Chef Story

As she watched the hibachi chef prepare her meal something seemed quite OFF. He swiftly sautéed her vegetables and chicken on the grill, but without warning, she felt her world was spinning. An unusual dizziness welled up in her thoughts and her mind. Yes, something seemed quite OFF!

She noticed a gentle sweet aroma in the room and she closed her eyes. A minute or two passed. With eyes wide open, she saw a mist all around the chef. He was totally unaware of what was happening. But was this really happening? The vertigo persisted and the smoky gray mist hovered over the chef like a cloud. No one else seemed aware of this. As if time was standing still, the mist slowly came into form. She saw a young man dressed in torn rags, with no shoes on his feet.

This apparition looked at HER, deep into her soul. Her heart was pounding but she couldn't turn her eyes from his. Suddenly, she felt completely at ease, and the spinning feeling left her. Each moment was permeated in slow motion....the hibachi chef and his movements and the people all around her. As the mist of a man drew near, she heard only his voice as his eyes pierced hers.

"Take heed of the souls oppressed and persecuted," he said.

Then she answered with her gentle spirit.

"What do you want me to do?"

With soft, loving eyes he looked at her.

"Be my voice, be my courage, be my compassion. Look! Your angels stand ready to guide you on your way!"

"Who are you?" she finally queried.

With a flash of light and unimaginable brightness all around him, his clothes turned to dazzling white. Angles surrounded him... celestial beings of joy and gladness. The light was so bright she closed her eyes. And when she opened them, a reverence lingered in the room, with all the people, with the chef, and with herself. Not a word was spoken. Utter stillness spread throughout the entire space. A dreamlike time was passing and without awareness the people slowly began their conversing again. The chef placed her steaming dish in front of her. She beamed with friendliness and the expression of tenderness in his eyes reminded her of the young man.

She would remember this day. She wanted to go home and write a poem about it. She would heed the words said to her because her angels stood ready to guide her on her way. She would honor each soul that crossed her path now and forevermore.

> "He who has compassion on the poor lends to the Lord, and he will repay him for his good deed."

> Proverbs 19: 17

Surrender To Nature

*D*o you have a favorite teacher in your life? I find myself grateful for the wisdom of my teachers. I was taught a method of true happiness several years ago. As an adult in school, we were given an unusual assignment. It was due in two weeks. We were to walk into a forest and go to the first tree we were drawn to. "Surrender to nature," our teacher explained. "Write any experience and feelings that come upon you. Stay in the forest by your tree until the time feels right to relinquish."

Thoughts of wasting precious time overcame me. I even thought of using my creative writing to make something up. But I changed my mind and set aside some time to find my tree.

It was a day of sunshine and warm breezes, so I went to a nearby park. When I stepped out of the car, I glanced to and fro at the many trees, really making an effort to be drawn to one particular tree. There it was! It stood at the riverbank; the tree was not very impressive at all, but I was drawn to it. As I approached my tree, I noticed three large nails protruding from its trunk. I immediately asked, "Did someone hurt you, too?" I thought about our Lord Jesus with three nails in His hands and feet. "Of all the trees in this entire park, I was drawn to you!" I said.

I spread my blanket on the ground near its trunk, sat down, and began to think of my many responsibilities, my problems, my future, my hurts and turmoil and the good wishes for my children. Time passed, and suddenly, I heard something. The tree branches above me were rustling in the breeze. It sounded so beautiful to me. These very trees were reflected in the river. I hadn't seen or heard this when I'd arrived! Next, I heard birds chirping and they landed at a close distance watching me. I saw a tiny ladybug crawling up a blade of grass in front of me. I peeked over the waters edge and saw some small fish swimming about. Squirrels playfully scampered from branch to branch in the tree across from me. I felt so at peace that my thoughts of distress didn't matter anymore. It seems my troubles just floated down the current of the river on a leaf as it passed by. It reminded me of a verse from the Psalms. "When cares abound within me, your comfort gladdens by soul." Psalm 94: 19

I never knew such an experience existed before. Here was the "find of a lifetime." True happiness filled my soul, my spirit and no one could take it from me. I said to my tree, "We may be damaged by life's cruel blows, but there is still peace and joy in the present." I was excited to get home and start writing my paper.

The following winter I visited my son in Boston. I took a walk and snowflakes were falling. I started off with a heavy heart. But the beautiful reality of my surroundings really turned my sadness to joy as I let go. I suddenly heard the sound of the ocean, I heard my own footsteps in the snow, and birds were singing, and the sound of wind chimes were in someone's yard. My black coat turned white and a pond had frozen into a smooth glass-like mirror. Peace and happiness were mine again.

I think God places teachers in our lives for a reason. And I think God doesn't want us to worry about anything. He wants us to be happy with all He has given us and trust Him completely. These experiences have made me very happy and I know for certain there are more to come.

"The earth has music for those who listen."

Unknown

To Make Their House A Home

Dave graduated from high school and the next day he was working with his Uncle Ernie delivering milk for Twin Pines Dairies. The young man was a quick learner, he dressed and ate before the sun got up; he was dependable and an honest worker.

Dave was with his buddies one Friday evening at the soda shop and he glanced at the door as SHE walked in. He couldn't breathe as he stared at Olivia, his high school sweetheart, although she was never aware of it. Her girlfriends slid in the booth next to his and she looked at him and waved a bit. His buddies gave him the business and he felt himself embarrassed and blushing.

Within two years, Dave had his own Twin Pines route and truck. He married Olivia and they moved into a lovely home on Agnes Street in Detroit. At Christmastime, many of Dave's customers had gifts for him left in their milk chutes. There were red and green packages with tags reading: "Dave our milkman." He received cookies, children's drawings, a pack of Lucky Strikes, even a home baked pie. When he came home from work, Olivia would be waiting on the front porch steps of their new home.

Their first son, Tim, was a climber and by eleven months old, he was climbing the stairway. He would peek out the top floor window smearing his little hand prints all over the glass. Dave and Olivia had two more children; a girl, Ella, then another boy, Glen. They did their homework at the big wooden kitchen table with Olivia's help. One evening the three of them were eating their bedtime snack of Cheerios and milk. They all heard a strange sound from the big oak table, even Dave. In the quiet of the house, all eyes were on that table. Then, ZAP! Out came a caterpillar as happy as can be. The children wanted to share their cereal with their little new friend but Olivia was aghast! Dave talked the little ones into letting the creature live outdoors where he belonged and the children reluctantly gave in. Dave had thought the warm coffee pot in the center of the table must have helped this caterpillar bore his way through. He wondered how long it had been there—it surely had its beginning in a tree—logs—2x4's—then remained trapped in the table!

In their dining room, Dave insisted on building a large wooden bookcase that covered the entire wall. The first treasured books for the family were encyclopedias dated 1951, the Revised Edition. Olivia was exceptionally pleased at the emphasis Dave gave to education. They were happy with their home and all their needs being met, all because of Dave's job at Twin Pines. In the winter, the children bundled up in their Twin Pines navy blue wool coats and in the summer, children's voices could be heard in the front of the house—"Red Rover, Red Rover, let Ella come over." Olivia gave them cups of Twin Pines chocolate milk as they lingered on the lawn looking for animals in the clouds.

Olivia hung pink flowered wallpaper in the foyer of their home and soon after, all the bedrooms were wallpapered too. One rainy Saturday afternoon, the children played hide'n seek and no one could find little Glen. Calls, shouts, and searching in every room proved unsuccessful. Olivia became concerned until she opened the linen closet door and found him fast asleep among the quilts and comforters. The family walked to St. Joseph Church one block down Agnes Street every Sunday, and Dave's children could always look forward to a bowl of Twin Pines ice cream after Sunday dinner.

Forty years later, there were good memories for aging Dave and Olivia as they drove past the well worn home they purchased so long ago. The fact it was still standing made them smile. They talked about the memories of the children growing up and all the work done to make their house a home.

> "Home is where love resides, memories are created, friends always belong, and laughter never ends."

Unknown

The Red Wagon

One of my earliest memories growing up in Detroit in the '50's was a beautiful summer day where flowers were blooming and the aroma of freshly mowed lawn was in the air. My brother, George, was nine years old, I was five and our baby sister was one.

George placed little Jane in our red wagon to take her for a ride down the block. Jane held her rag doll tightly as if *she* might enjoy a ride too. I placed my little hands on the back of the wagon and started to push. George had the handle and ran as fast as he could. We were really flying and the baby was giggling with glee. I was pushing much too hard and suddenly George fell to the cement. He was wearing shorts, knees exposed to the rough sidewalk. I can still see in my minds' eye my brother's blood running down his legs.

We all got ourselves into the house in a panic where mom placed George on the commode and cleaned up the bloody mess and applied clean bandages. I watched as George cried crocodile tears moaning in pain as mother worked. I felt so sad, I started to cry too. I remember saying over and over, "I'm sorry, George, I'm sorry!"

I knew in my five year old heart that if I hadn't pushed so hard this never would have happened. George finally stopped crying like a light switch turning off.

He looked me right in the eye and said to me, "It's ok, Mary, I'm all right."

Those words were more soothing than the medicinal cream on his knees at that moment. I was always very careful after that not to push the wagon too hard. I think children instinctively know what other children are feeling.

> "If you push too hard against anything, you get the opposite of what you want."

(from a movie called, *Three Wishes.*)

QUESTIONS

Sometimes I have such profound questions,
And I want to know the answers right now!
But it appears that just in the asking
The answers all melt away
And it's not that important any more.
But there are good questions that make me ponder—
Such as "What do I believe and why?"
And "What does it mean to love someone?"
There are good questions that keep me from intruding
Like… "Who owns the problem?"
Some people need to figure out all on their own
How to solve their problem.
Once they do, their own dignity comes forth.
But God, Can I give a little advice if I have a really good answer?
Will they listen? When do I let go? What about my experience, Lord?
Dear God, I know very well you love me
And you certainly love my questions
For they are from You.
A question like: "What do you want to prayerfully and peacefully change?"
(I must remember now, I can only change myself!)
I want to let selfishness and fear pass me by
And just do my best in all I try to accomplish.
If I fail, then let it be a learning lesson for the next time I try.
And in that failure, I would still treat myself very kindly
For that is when I am so vulnerable.
That is when I need most to be treated kindly.
Isn't that part of loving someone?

And didn't Christ say, "Love your neighbor <u>*as yourself*</u>?"
What is *so* important to me?
Most folks answer "family and health".
It is important that God help me see clearly
What my call is.
It is important to me that people feel safe with me.
It is important to me that I genuinely affirm people
For that is what unlocks their capacity to see their value.
My dear loving Friend and Lord,
Always hold me close to you.
There is **NO QUESTION** you will not answer.

"I love You, O Lord
 My Friend forever
 My Peace
 My Comforter
 My Safety
 You are all I need
 You are my Teacher
 You have supported me during my hurts and trials
 And changed me to be patient waiting for You
 Always turning to You. Amen."

A Psalm by Mary Cole

Happy

"A happy heart does good like a medicine and a cheerful mind brings healing." (Proverbs 17:22)

I have discovered that different age groups have very different ideas of happiness. Little children say that <u>candy</u> makes them happy. My three year old grandson said, "My mommy and daddy make me happy!"

Children also say that summer vacation and being free from school makes them happy. I asked a thirty year old woman what are some of the things that makes a person happy. She responded with a question of her own.

"What "SHOULD" or what "DOES"? She sees her friends buying things to make them happy. She watches the comparing of who owns the most good stuff as a reason for happiness. Her own idea was different—she likes a quiet day at home to just BE, hanging out with her husband and kids. I asked a grandmother what made her happy.

She said, "Hugging my two grandsons makes me happy!" Another grandmother said, "Hearing my kids together laughing and laughing makes me happy."

As a seasoned adult, I tend to look within the heart. Here is my own version of some of the things that makes a person happy.

When another human being honors what is important to another. That includes rapt attention at discussion of topics.

Happy

Doing a Millie Ernst can make a person happy. Who is Millie Ernst you may ask? When I worked at the Senior Citizens Center, she was a regular visitor. Millie had been in a car accident that left her crippled but she joined every activity possible and was present at every party and class. When she walked down the hall with her cane, she talked to herself. "C'mon ole' girl, you are doing fine. You are gonna do great in that class." She was determined to live in the moment and not in the past. I loved Millie. She was the first person I have ever met that really lived in the here and now. Because of Millie, I am able to use this technique painting outdoors. I can enjoy the stroke of the brush, the birds chirping, the breeze on my cheeks and the lemonade flavor on my lips.

It's a happy person who is satisfied with the way things are and that includes dropping unreasonable expectations, from life, from others, from self.

Sharing and giving of our talents and time is a recipe for happiness. The giving of attention to another searching soul meets our own need for attention as well.

We can still be happy even if we don't receive what we prefer. We can concentrate on what we DO have and sometimes we have to wait. While waiting for one thing to happen—we can do something else instead of getting all ruffled feathers and causing havoc for the people around us just because we have to wait.

Practicing forgiveness of others and self is a good way to maintain happiness.

Singing, spontaneous dancing, and musical instruments can change peoples' attitudes in a hurry. The music I love always brings me much happiness.

One can be an instrument of spreading happiness. If we want children to improve let them hear the nice things we say about them to others. I guess that could be applied to people of any age!

And so, happiness can be improved by practicing it daily and it is a voluntary state that we can actually develop. We can concentrate on happy thoughts because we are very much in control of our own minds!

"Most people are about as happy as they make up their minds to be." Abraham Lincoln. So what makes *you* happy?

> "Shout for joy, O heavens, rejoice O earth. Burst into song, O mountains! For the Lord comforts his people and will have compassion on his afflicted ones."
>
> Isaiah 49: 13

On That Summer Night

On that summer night of the full moon, I was alone on the beach. I sat Indian style on my old blanket and it was dark all about me in spite of the moon and billions of stars above. I had collected twigs, dried leaves and driftwood earlier in the day placing it all in the fire pit.

It was amazing to me to experience the gentile pulsing of my own heart as I started to light the fire. I could see and hear the lapping of the waves at the shore and it seemed to synchronize with my heartbeat. Peace filled me.

All the cabins to the north of me appeared quiet and empty that night. Further down the beach was a secret cove. The sand was so smooth from the waves' cleansing and contained tiny sea shells that pricked the bottom of ones feet.

As I sat staring at the fire, I realized I couldn't see the beautiful rock creation I made on the sand the day before. My eyes adjusted to the darkness but soon they were burning from the smoke so I moved my blanket to the other side of the fire. Then I heard a still small voice.

"Get up." There was urgency in that voice. I was perplexed and scratched my head. For some reason, my armpits were soaked with perspiration and my heart began to pound.

"Get up!" I heard the voice again only this time my body leaped off the blanket and then I saw it! Hurling through space in the sky above was a bright fireball like a falling star. The hissing sound in the air startled me and I ran as fast as I could down the beach.

Kaboom! It hit the earth! I glanced back and looked up in the sky worried there might be another object. I felt myself begin to tremble from head to foot. Slowly I walked back to my campfire and found a rock-like substance from the universe which had burned a crater in the middle of my blanket! It was a meteorite—an honest to goodness meteorite. My thoughts were racing backward as I remembered the voice of warning. "THANK YOU," I shouted, and the echo permeated the lake front.

I went to bed that night leaving the beach as it was. My legs jumped and fluttered all night as I tried to sleep. But in the morning, I told my story to a neighbor as we sipped our coffee in lounge chairs by the shore. Her comment was insightful.

"It seems God revealed his thoughts to you last night. I'm so glad he did!"

Note: Meteorites are made of iron and nickel and are very heavy. Meteorites are always named for the places they were found usually a nearby town or after the person who was struck by it—(like Ann Hodges)

> "He who forms the mountains, creates the wind, and reveals his thoughts to man, he who turns dawn to darkness, and treads the high places of the earth—the Lord God Almighty is his Name."
> Amos 4: 13

Books By Jane

I have so many fond memories of my brothers and sisters growing up in Detroit in the 1950's. I remember feeling so proud and happy to have Jane as my very own little sister. Our parents allowed us to have friends over and play for hours in our bungalow basement. We had a chalkboard, records, games, little dishes and puppets and plenty of books. One summer day, my friends and I were playing with our dolls in the backyard, but Jane and her friends decided to play in the basement. Now, this day would be unlike any other.

Having a brother who was an elementary school teacher gave our dad the opportunity to receive many used books. He meticulously built book shelves to cover an entire wall in the basement. As time went on, we accumulated prose and poetry books, history, math, and geography, English as well as encyclopedias, novels and religious books.

Dad always told us, "If you want to know something, you can always find it in a book."

I can actually say I felt that my dad honored books and honored education and so, being an organized person he labeled each section of books according to their category.

Seven year old Jane and her friends came upon a wonderful idea that day. They decided to arrange all the books by the color of its cover! Hours and hours of work were accomplished by a few sincere children. The red books were on the top shelf, the blue books were underneath. On the third shelf black and brown covered books were placed. There were plenty of green books so the fourth shelf contained these. On and on the work continued.

When dad got home from work, smiling Jane took his hand and led him to her surprise. I can still see the look on my dad's face when he first laid eyes on the bookshelves. When mom came downstairs at dad's beckon, her shriek gave Jane a jolt.

My parents were kind and tried to explain to my sister they wouldn't be able to find a history book or a poetry book because the books were all mixed up. But in Jane's way of thinking they were organized beautifully.

That evening mom and dad climbed into bed at 2am and the books were back where they belonged. Needless to say, Jane was very disappointed her work wasn't appreciated and my heart was broken for her. But after time passed, it was all forgotten and the children returned day after day happily playing with dolls and games and puppets and books.

> "Children have one kind of silliness, as you know, and grown-ups have another kind."
>
> C.S. Lewis

THE DAY OF WHITES

The day began like any other—but Cathy could never have imagined how it would end. She threw back the covers, got up and turned off the alarm. The years of her nursing career were over; she attended college now, a dream come true. Cathy staggered into the kitchen to make some mocha cinnamon flavored coffee. Oh, the aroma of the delicious brew gave her that spark to start her day. She cut up some apple slices, made some peanut butter toast, got dressed and off to the university she went.

Cathy played inspirational music as she drove and sipped her hot coffee. The bridge over the expressway had just been reconstructed with a fenced-in walkway for pedestrians.

"Wow!" screamed Cathy, "I can't believe this!"

Little white cups had been stuck in the fence above the expressway that read these words, "I LOVE U CATHY."

"Oh, Lord! Who put those white cups in the fence? Is it *me* someone loves? Could it be *me*?"

A thought just occurred to Cathy as she drove. *All the Cathy's who drive by today will see that sign and freak out like I did. Will they all be wondering if the sign was meant for them?*

"White as Snow" was playing on her CD as she sang and drove happily along. Cathy looked up and saw falling from the sky white Styrofoam packing material. It reminded her of popcorn.

The Day of Whites

She said, "That's weird, it looks like it's snowing! Where is all this stuff coming from?"

She drove fifteen miles and the little white pieces just kept falling. The song seemed a facsimile for the gently falling white fluff.

Cathy pulled into the university parking garage, opened her door and the first thing she saw on the ground was one of those white packing materials.

What a puzzling circumstance, she thought. She carefully picked up the bit of "snow" and placed it in her glove box.

Cathy met her friend Tracey as they entered the astronomy class. She told Tracey all about the white cups stuck in the fence and the white packing material falling from the sky as she drove downtown. "I didn't see anything driving to school," said Tracey.

Their professor demanded quiet and started explaining the fundamentals of the White Dwarf Stars.

"The first detected White Dwarf in 1862 is called Sirius B. White Dwarfs are dying stars and 7% of them are closest to the sun."

Cathy whispered to her friend, "White Dwarfs remind me of this morning on the expressway."

Tracey just gave her a strange look.

"The super giants, like Betelgeuse", continued the professor, "has a diameter the distance between our sun and Jupiter!"

Cathy's hand was hurting from taking notes as she closed her book after class.

Her favorite place on campus was the art department. <u>Color and Design 2</u> was next and she looked forward to the unusual assignments from this eccentric professor.

One of the students was showing off her new tattoo of a large dragon on her abdomen when the professor walked in.

"Your assignment for next week is to create an abstract design using only white materials. You may use fabrics, white plastic bags, white napkins, anything at all that is on this planet, only it must be white. Your artwork must be suitable for hanging, and the clincher-—a poem must be written in explanation of your project."

Cathy was just stunned as she heard the requirements.

More white stuff, she thought.

The day was drawing to a close. As Cathy drove home she got a phone call on her cell from her sister.

"Hey, Cath, I'm stopping over after work tonight. I bought you some white coconut candles on sale on my lunch hour today. I know how you like them. See you later. Bye." *Unbelievable!* She thought.

Cathy went to bed that evening wondering about her "white" eventful day! She dozed off peacefully. For some strange reason she woke up and opened her eyes. There hovering above her (about two feet) was a bright, white, glowing angel looking at her. His hair was dazzling white—short and in rolls on his head with the style similar to the wigs men wore in the 1780's. His robe-like clothes were perfect bright white and she saw a glowing mist all about him. She had never seen a white like this on planet earth!

As they looked at one another she gasped, *"OH!"* He actually had a look of concern on his face that he had been seen. It was something like—*"uh oh, she wasn't supposed to see me."* Cathy thought maybe he would linger above her a little longer if she didn't gasp like that. She thought about his hair in rolls so dazzling white.

She thought God was trying to tell her, *"Go ahead and believe in angels, they're real."* She realized she was given a wonderful gift that she would always remember. *Perhaps on my dying day I will meet this angel again*, she pondered. When Cathy was a nurse caring for the dying, some patients told her about the angels they saw just waiting for them. She thought that life is filled with amazing circumstances if we just open our eyes and believe!

Whenever Cathy thought of that day she wondered if it was all a dream. But then one day she remembered to check her glove box.

> "I have heard there are particles of the universe inside each one of us. There is majestic balance in the universe. There is brilliance and beauty in the universe. And it's our God and Creator who MADE the universe. And He made you and me to discover all there is to see."
>
> Mary Cole

Clara Gilmore

*I*t was a cool fall afternoon when Clara Gilmore finished her routine workload. Bessie was milked, the chickens were fed, and a modest meal of bread, meat and greens from the garden was prepared. It was eaten in haste because a photographer had come to town and her children insisted on having a photo taken of her.

She carefully placed her hand-made calico dress over her head. She was grateful for her trundle sewing machine. It had been a friend when times were sparse. A little extra income was welcomed as she repaired trousers, dresses and shirts for folks in her community. The lace around the collar of her dress had been a piece she removed from her own mothers' threadbare frock. She gently tied her kerchief around her head and proceeded to walk the two miles to town. Clara's husband had died ten years prior but she continued to work hard on the small farm they owned in Illinois. It wouldn't be much longer. Her heart had been speaking to her about a welcome change that was coming soon.

Her thoughts wandered as she slowly walked down the familiar road.

"I'm so relieved that my sons finished the wood chopping for me. Winter's blast will be here soon, but I have more than enough now to keep me warm till April. I have plenty of yarn to knit several baby afghans this winter, too. I hope these arthritic fingers hold up. Dear Lord, there are new babies coming into your world and I pray they are healthy and happy but, honestly, I'm in a quandary, Lord. Can I make it through another winter alone? I trust in your provision, but I'm still afraid. It's the routine; getting up, doing chores, eating, cleaning, going to bed and over and over and over again. It takes so long for spring to come! I feel so alone!"

The fragrance of fall was in the air. She watched the swaying, golden trees. A breeze touched her face very gently and then she remembered her past clearly. A flock of sparrows chirped in unison down the road and a special peace permeated her soul.

Yes, Clara remembered her life as a little girl. Her mama and papa worked each day of their lives to sustain their family. Clara was the oldest of seven children, always taking responsibility for teaching her younger siblings. As a young woman, she learned midwifery, which was a bittersweet experience because some babies didn't survive. But no one blamed Clara. Her reputation was one of honor and trust. She fell in love and married strong Edmund, who was strict and dedicated to hard work. Life was tragic when she lost three of her babies to cholera. And yet, gratefully, three sons survived the outbreak. Her eldest son, Louis, became a prominent doctor following in his mother's footsteps and Arthur became a railroad engineer. He told many stories of adventure and danger when he came to visit at Christmastime. Albert maintained the general store in town with the help of his wife and children. It had been a full life, full of giving, not asking for anything in return.

Clara was greeted by a neighbor lady on the road.

"Hello there! It's a fine day! I've just returned from Albert's store and, today, he received some fine bolts of calico cottons. Are you off to see him?"

Clara felt weary at the thought of cutting and sewing another dress so she dismissed her neighbor's question and said, "The photographer is in town. My children don't want to forget what I look like!"

In Clara's way of thinking, there was always time for a little humor. Her neighbor laughed and with a nod went on her way.

Clara arrived in town and waved to her son, Albert, who was sweeping the steps of the store. A large sign caught her eye, *GET YOUR PICTURE TAKEN HERE*. As she entered the photographer's small room, she noticed the group of children standing like little statues. POOF! They all blinked and laughed in unison. "Washington Township Grade School #20," noted the photographer. It was Clara's turn. Albert entered and gave his ma a wink. POOF! "Clara Gilmore #21." The deed was done.

Clara and Albert walked arm in arm to the store. She looked over the beautiful calicos but felt she wouldn't have time for much sewing. Albert handed to her a basket of fresh tomatoes, parsley, butternut squash and apples. She thanked him and began her walk home.

Clara returned to her deep thoughts. "Lord, I'm sure now of this welcome change you keep gently bringing to my mind." Her world suddenly became alive, invigorating and yet very calming. She took in a deep breath as she looked up at the majestic sky. Clara felt an ache, a sharp pain and she was gone. The apples gently rolled from her basket and touched her lifeless hand. Clara's welcomed change had come.

> "My sheep hear my voice. I know them and they follow me. I give them eternal life and they shall never perish. No one shall snatch them out of my hand."
>
> John 10: 27, 28

Free

*I*t was a chilly fall day in Michigan. Mark and Scott, two eight year old buddies, were in the back seat of the car and mom was driving. The radio was playing and the boys were a little hyper from nibbling on sweet Kit Kats. Suddenly, without warning, the boys both shouted,

"Stop the car! Mom, stop, please stop the car!"

"What on earth? What's wrong?" said mom as she slowed to a crawl.

"There's a sign mom! A sign!"

It says, "free puppies!"

"Please mom, we just want to *look* at the puppies. P L E E E A S E!"

It was Saturday afternoon. Dad was out of town for the entire week. There was really no reason why mom couldn't stop. But her words to the boys were careful.

"We are not, I repeat, NOT taking a puppy home."

"Ok mom, we won't. We just want to *see* the puppies."

Mom pulled in the driveway and saw the sign for herself—it was handmade on cardboard in big wobbly first grade letters: **FREE PUPPIES.**

❧ Free ❧

As soon as they got out of the car, they were greeted by a welcoming family. "Only one puppy left," said the mother.

"Oh dear", said mom, as her heart began to race.

The woman handed Mark the last puppy. Love filled his eyes as he glanced at mom. It was a black lab and a male puppy. He had huge paws, only eight weeks old, sweet and gentle, needy and playful. But within minutes the puppy fell asleep in Mark's arms. The black bundle enveloped Mark's red down filled jacket and he begged, "Please can I keep him, mom?"

Scott already had a dog. He urged Mark to beg a little more. Mom caved in. She felt like she wanted the pup too.

That was the day Brute joined the family. What an exciting first night it was for all of them! Dad came home after a week of puppy life. What a surprise for dad but, like Mark, he had just one look…

As Brute grew, his true personality would shine. He had the most unusual behavior every time mom vacuumed the stairway. She started vacuuming at the bottom and went up. Brute would sprawl across the entire stair *above* the stair she was working on. He would stretch one paw downward. Was he attempting to see if his paw would get vacuumed up too?

Mom would say, "I'm gonna get you Brute."

Then he'd jerk his paw up and sprawl his body out on the next stair above as comfortable as you please. All the way up, the paw would sneak down—mom would say her little ditty and up he'd go to the next stair.

This amazing dog was with the family for many years and finally passed away while Mark was attending Northern Michigan University. Brute was free and dearly loved.

> "A dog may be man's best friend, but a child's best friend is a puppy."
>
> Unknown

Picture Walk

The roaring fire and sounds of crickets were just a memory now. She had a quiet evening sitting at the waters' edge the night before. But this morning, the lake looked like glass and not a leaf was stirring. It was very still and the air was chilly. She looked up at the blue, blue sky—not a hint of a cloud anywhere. She decided to go for a walk and heard falling acorns upon the roofs of homes and cottages. She also heard "kerplunk" in the lake where the acorns dropped.

So many bird calls astounded her as she watched these cherubs dart from branch to branch. Then the chipmunks chirped as they scampered to hide from her underneath the docks brought to land. She smiled. She felt like someone was walking behind her so she turned around and saw a beautiful black lab give her a smile of its own. What a joy to pet this gentle animal and watch him walk away seemingly satisfied with the attention she gave.

Walking on, she felt the soft touch of a passing cob web on her cheek. Was it a cob web or perhaps an angels' kiss? She picked up a few unique maple leaves and saw beauty in each one all displaying their own particular color. The lake was so still; not a bit of lapping waves at the shore.

And then she noticed little purple wildflowers growing along the path. They reached high basking in the warm sunshine. Leaves were falling, falling, gliding slowly until they reached the ground. A woodpecker was viciously chipping away the bark of a tree. She watched him peck the bits of wood. They were flying to and fro and she saw a little pile of fresh pieces of bark on the exposed roots of the soil. Her eyes spotted a rock on the ground. It was indeed unique, a perfect heart shape and she planned to put it on her dresser at home. There were many aromas in the morning air; smoky simmering embers of the campfires, someone cooking bacon, and the familiar skunk spray in the distance.

"Something frightened the animal", she thought.

A hungry feeling made her turn back, and as she retraced her steps, she passed the purple wildflowers. She noticed someone had created a little path of rocks leading to the shore.

"That must have taken a strong arm and a days' worth of work", she pondered.

Soon she would be home. She smiled again thinking "what a peaceful day. Thank you Creator of all things wonderful."

> "You give drink to every beast of the field. Beside them the birds of heaven dwell from among the branches they send forth their song. You water the mountains from your palace. The earth is abundant with the fruit of your works.
>
> Psalm 104: 12, 13

A Plate of Cookies

Sue's doorbell rang one late March afternoon
"Now what?" She moaned in exasperation.
All she saw was a plate of cookies.
"I wonder who?" She whispered in contemplation.

"Mmmm! Lemon, my favorite," She said aloud.
Sue ate them ALL, then noticed the old plate.
I'll fill this relic with gingersnaps
For *Jane's* front porch—her amusement to escalate!

When Jane received her gift of pleasure,
Her kitchen hummed with "date nut oatmeal"
"I'll surprise Debbie and use this old plate."
So *Deb* opened *her* door and gave a happy squeal.

Around the neighborhood the old plate went
Filled with cookies and making heads scratch.
There was Linda, Marie, Phyllis and Peg,
Until one day Sue hosted a coffee clatch.

With laughter infectious, the women queried-
"Who started the tradition of BAKE, PLATE AND HIDE?"
All became silent, waiting in anticipation-
Jane roared, "Speak up, guilty one, don't be tongue tied!"

"Can someone at least *claim* the old plate?"
A soft voice was heard, "My great aunt Babette
Gave me the dish when I was just eight."
Auntie said, "Always share, my dear Claudette."

So, dear Claudette remembered the words
And began the frolic extraordinary.
Many smiling women went home that day
With their stories of Claudette's tributary.

"Do good. Be rich in good deeds and be generous and willing to share."

1 Timothy 6: 18

Grandchildren

$\mathcal{I}$ am a grandmother and really enjoy telling stories about my grandchildren. And why not? These little ones say and do the dearest things and their sweet conversations have stayed fresh in my memory. I loved reading books to them, painting, making snowmen and snow angels, playing with legos, play dough and Lincoln logs, crafts at the kitchen table and, of course, singing with my grandchildren.

One beautiful sunny day in May, I took my grandson for a stroller ride—trucks always caught his eye.

"There's a 4x4 gamma! He shouted. Then we saw a robin on the grass.

"Let's go get the robin, gamma, faster, faster."

Naturally, the robin flew across the street. We tried this again and again. And I started to think the robin was actually playing a game with us! We decided to go in the backyard and the robin seemed to follow us.

My grandson whispered to me, "Let's go get the robin."

We walked slowly, closer and closer. The robin looked right at us and started to walk toward us! It's true! This beautiful bird was about three feet away from us. It seemed like such a long time and my little grandson was acutely aware of this mysterious event. He looked at me with wonder in his eyes. Until finally, the robin looked at us both and flew away as if to say,

"That was fun! Hope to see you again some day!"

~~~~~~~

This little boy always enjoyed a day of painting. On this day, he used all the colors in the rainbow—a picture for his mama. There were bits of green, lots of purple, red, pink and blue. He had such fun cleaning the brushes in the large cup on the table. The water turned into a deep brown color. He shouted out to me, "Ok gamma, your coffee is ready!"

And he laughed and laughed at his own joke.

A large snowstorm was coming upon us. I told my granddaughter the weatherman said we could get a foot of snow—maybe even two feet!

Then grandpa came over for a visit and she said to him,

"Grandpa, we're gonna get a shoe of snow—maybe even two shoes!"

~~~~~~~

Children love to play in big boxes. My granddaughter was having so much fun with a large box on my kitchen floor, but suddenly, she slipped and fell down face first. I felt so sad because she cried and cried, so I held her as I sat on the floor with my legs outstretched. I told her when I was little, I fell down the stairs at my house and my brother and my daddy put me in the car to take me to the hospital. I was crying so hard! As we were driving I stopped crying and I told them I was "all right" so they drove back home. She listened very intently. Then she noticed that I had two different socks on my feet!

I said, "What a silly grandma I am, let's go upstairs and find socks that are a match.

"OK", she said with a smile as I wiped the tears off her cheek.

⇾ Grandchildren ⇽

We cleaned up my messy sock drawer and finally found the sock to match. My granddaughter told me to sit on the chair and then she began to pull off the wrong sock. What a surprise this was to me! She actually put the correct sock on my foot all by herself at 3 years old. My eyes filled up with tears of love.

And then she said, "This is how my daddy puts my socks on."

Her dreadful fall and her many tears were all forgotten.

~~~~~~~

Once my grandson and his dad came for a visit. I entertained this dear boy while grandpa and son worked on a project. I got the birthday cake play dough out with rolling pin and tools and pretend candies. Then we played with the Lincoln logs on the living room floor, we painted with poster paints, had a snack and some grape juice—it was time to go so I packed him a container of watermelon chunks for the car ride home. BYE BYE!

Hugs and kisses were given and off they went in the car.

I started to put things away and the doorbell rang. It was my grandson and his daddy.

I said, "Did you forget something?"

"Yes," he said.

I waited a bit and he looked up at his dad. He was given a nod and finally my grandson said, "I love you grandma!"

Another hug was given and a "I love you too."

This is called PURE LOVE.

To all my grandchildren:

"I may not see you or talk to you every day but I think of you and love you every day."

What Is Forever?

*T*houghts and different ideas of "what is forever" have been racing around in my head for days now. My list is growing steadily…

They say those plastic bags do not disintegrate in the landfills as well as plastic disposable diapers. Will they still be intact in a billion years? And yet, a billion years from now isn't forever.

Perhaps pieces of the exploded space capsules will be found in the universe forever. But wouldn't the cold or the black holes make the stuff disappear eventually?

And what about the seasons of summer, fall, winter and spring? Won't they keep their routine on earth like they have since time began? This leads me to the earth itself; will there be an end to earth someday? The words of scripture talk about the new heavens and new earth so perhaps our earth as we know it isn't "forever." If gold and silver has been around since the world began, could gold and silver and other elements last forever? I think not if the earth is gone. But what about these elements existing on other planets? Will our universe live forever?

And there is the subject of us people. Aren't people going to be around forever? Of course, we'd have to have the earth to live on. Scientists say the planets are uninhabitable. I'm back to the drawing board—thinking—pondering.

I'm beginning to believe what is forever is not an object one can hold or even see with the eye. It is something much deeper, more profound and continuously and perfectly stable. I was reading scripture the other day and found that "God's mercy endures forever."

A different interpretation says, "God's love endures forever.

As I searched a little more I found, "His kindness endures forever," "The Lord shall reign forever," "The fidelity of the Lord endures forever."

I looked up "fidelity"—(strict observance of One's promises.) It was comforting to also read "The grass withers, and flower wilts but the Word of the Lord stands forever."

It looks like God's promises are the real deal. John wrote: "In truth, I love each of you—this love is based on the truth that abides in us and will be with us forever."

So, mercy, love, kindness, the Lord Himself, His fidelity, His Word and truth live forever. Thanks be to God!

> "But my salvation will last forever, my righteousness
> will never fail."
>
> Isaiah 51: 6c

Lightning Source UK Ltd.
Milton Keynes UK
UKHW021300121120
373269UK00009B/247